# God Isn't Complicated

AN INTERACTIVE WORKBOOK BY
ALYSSA RUETER

**God Isn't Complicated**

Copyright © 2026 by Alyssa Rueter

Published by Lucid Books in Houston, TX

www.LucidBooks.com

All rights reserved. No part of this publication may be reproduced, stored in a retrieval system, or transmitted in any form by any means, electronic, mechanical, photocopy, recording, or otherwise, without the prior permission of the publisher, except as provided for by USA copyright law.

Unless otherwise indicated, scripture quotations are taken from the (NIV) Holy Bible, New International Version®, NIV®. Copyright ©1973, 1978, 1984, 2011 by Biblica, Inc.™ Used by permission of Zondervan. All rights reserved worldwide. www.zondervan.com The "NIV" and "New International Version" are trademarks registered in the United States Patent and Trademark Office by Biblica, Inc.™

Scripture quotations marked (AMP) are taken from the Amplified Bible. Copyright © 1954, 1958, 1962, 1964, 1965, 1987 by The Lockman Foundation, La Habra, CA. All rights reserved. Used by Permission.

Scripture quotations marked (BSB) are taken from The Holy Bible, Berean Standard Bible, BSB. Copyright © 2021 Berean Standard Bible. All rights reserved.

Scripture quotations marked (ESV) are taken from the ESV® Bible (The Holy Bible, English Standard Version®), copyright © 2001 by Crossway, a publishing ministry of Good News Publishers. Used by permission. All rights reserved.

Scripture quotations marked (NKJV) are taken from the New King James Version®. Copyright © 1982 by Thomas Nelson. Used by permission. All rights reserved.

eISBN: 978-1-63296-838-8
ISBN: 978-1-63296-837-1

Special Sales: Most Lucid Books titles are available in special quantity discounts. Custom imprinting or excerpting can also be done to fit special needs. Contact Lucid Books at Info@LucidBooks.com

*To Yia-yia Schmelzer and Gail Uskert,*
*who continually spoke God's life to me, thank you.*

# Table of Contents

### 1. Pray — 9
This is so crucial to the Christian life, but do we take it seriously? A list of verses has been given for review.

### 2. Believe — 17
Do you have full assurance in your faith?

### 3. Precious — 23
Do you see yourself as precious? Review of Isaiah 43:4.

### 4. Set — 27
What do you think about during your day? That can really affect how you act. Review of Colossians 3:2.

### 5. Transformed — 31
What do our lives say about God? Review of Romans 12:1-2.

### 6. Know — 35
Did you realize what a privileged it is that God says we can know Him?! Review of John 17:3.

### 7. God is Our Father — 39
It wasn't just stated once, but SEVERAL times. A list of verses has been provided for individual review. Really think, do you see God as our Father?

### 8. Cares — 43
You wouldn't be human if you didn't have cares. God addresses that; he wants to help us with it! Review of Matthew 6:31-34.

### 9. God. Only God. — 47
He wants us to be His and His alone. Review of Exodus 20: 2-3.

### 10. All-Powerful — 51
We have a God who is all-powerful. Take a moment. What does that even mean? Review of Jeremiah 32:27.

### 11. Sustain — 55
What does that mean? Have you ever looked at what that doesn't mean? You will really enjoy knowing that God sustains us. Review of Hebrews 1:3.

### 12. Flee — 59
What are we running from or running towards? Review of 2 Timothy 2:22.

### 13. Abound in Hope — 63
That doesn't mean maintain or get just what you need. God wants us to abound. Review of Romans 15:13.

### 14. Unite — 67
To be united with Christ—that's a thing!! Review of Ephesians 1:7-10.

### 16. Seek — 71
What does it mean to seek? Is that something that you currently do? Review of Matthew 6:33.

### 16. Life — 75
God wants to share life with us, but first, we must stop acting in sin. Review of Romans 8:13.

### 17. Refreshing — 79
Who needs to be refreshed? God tells us the way. Review of Psalms of Psalms 19:7.

### 18. Strength — 83
Have you ever felt like you can't do anymore? Well great news, God wants to be our strength. Review of verses for prayer and meditation.

### 19. Trust — 87
Think, do you really trust God? What happens when we trust Him? Review of Psalms 28:7.

### 20. Cast — 91
That's an action verb. We are to cast our anxieties on God, but do we? Review of 1 Peter 5:7.

### 21. Shaken — 95
Do you want to feel confident? Well, God tells us that He won't let the righteous be shaken. Review of Psalms 55:22.

### 22. Peace — 99
Who wants peace? Do you really see peace in your life or the opposite of that? Review of Philippians 4:4-7.

### 23. Focus — 103
God doesn't just want to offer us peace. He wants us to be perfectly peaceful. The craziest part is we don't have to jump through hoops to get there. Review of Isaiah 26:3.

### 24. Watch Preserve — 107
Preserve. The God of the universe doesn't just want us to worship Him; he wants to take care of us. Review of Psalms 121:8.

### 25. Restores — 111
Not to harm but to heal; that is what God is about. Review of Psalms 23:3.

### 26. Faithful — 115
God is faithful. Have you ever really thought about that? Have you really accepted this in your heart? Review of verses for prayer and meditation.

### 27. Priceless — 119
Have you ever heard yourself described as priceless? Well, God calls us just that. Review of Psalms 36:7.

### 28. Compared to God — 125
We say this. Do we live like this? A list of verses for prayer and meditation.

### 29. Plan — 129
God created you and has a plan for your life. We heard it, but now let's take time to talk with Him about it. Review of verses for prayer and meditation.

### 30. Prosper — 133
We all want to prosper. Good news: God has a plan for us to prosper. Review of Jeremiah 29:11

### 31. Abandon — 137
Have you looked at what this means and doesn't mean? God won't abandon us! Review of Hebrews 13:5.

### 32. To be Afraid — 141
What does it mean to be afraid? How should we then act in our daily lives? Review of Hebrews 13:6.

### 33. It is good — 147
It is good to be near to God. We have been given the privilege to draw near to God, the god of the universe! Review of Psalms 73:28.

### 34. His Divine power — 151
Did you know that God gives us divine power to aid us in our lives?! Let's talk about it! Review of 2 Peter 1:3.

### 35. Rejoice, Pray, & Give Thanks — 155
Simple instructions given to Christians on how to live. Review of 1 Thessalonians 5:16-18.

### 36. Be still — 159
How often do we just stop to be still? This is a great time to think and meditate on those two words. A list of verses has been provided for review.

**CHAPTER 1**
# PRAY

Pray. P.R.A.Y. Pray!!

# Pray

**Definition** Pray

**Definition** Request

PRAY.
P.R.A.Y.
PRAY!!!

## Pray.

Hopefully, you looked up the definition of pray and request. Did you find anything interesting about the definitions?

Now, look up the antonyms (opposites) of pray and request and write it over here.

**Think about how you pray.**

Does your prayer reflect a positive faith in the King of All? Do you pray with demands?

**I want you to take time and consider:**

Do you recognize that you are addressing the Almighty God when you pray? Is it about God's will, or is it about your will to be done?

Antonyms — Pray

Antonyms — Request

Do not treat prayer as the wish list or grocery list of things you need. See prayer as a way to lay it all before God, to confess that He is in control. Remember, Jesus prayed. Yes! **Jesus, while on earth, felt the need to pray** (Matthew 14:23, 26:36; Mark 1:35, 6:46; Luke 5:16, 6:12). The night Jesus was betrayed, we are told He went to pray three separate times (Matthew 26:44). Three times!

Do you know what Jesus did at the end of His life when He was being put on the cross? He prayed for everyone around Him! Prayed. He asked that God forgive them (Luke 23:34). What a beautiful picture of love. He was praying for the sinners when He could have been complaining or telling them how it was really going down. **If Jesus felt the need to pray, why would we not also pray?!**

God calls us to pray. That should sound almost unbelievable to us. The God of the universe wants to hear from us! Shouldn't we be running to this opportunity as often as we are able?

God answered the prayers of believers so many times in the Bible. Prayer changes us. Praying keeps us humble and reliant on God, who is our strength (Nehemiah 8:10; Isaiah 12:2, 40:29, 41:10; 1 Peter 5:10).

**Choose a few verses to write out:**

People who were stressed were delivered because they cried out to God. It's as simple as that (Psalms 107:28). The Bible also states that we, too, can receive what we ask for if we pray in faith (Matthew 21:22; John 14:13-14).

> Prayer is admitting we are not in control. It means we are trusting God and His timing time.

Give Him time. Be honest with yourself now. Is there anything you lack? Maybe something you want to add to your prayers?

_____
_____
_____
_____
_____
_____

> Food for thought: Can you know someone without talking? This is why we need prayer!

Take time to review these verses. Choose a few that stand out. This is a great time to pray these verses to God. Ask Him for help if there is unbelief. Ask Him to make the verse a reality in your life.

| | |
|---|---|
| **2 Chronicles 7:14** | **Ephesians 6:18** |
| **James 5:14** | **Mark 11:24** |
| **Matthew 5:44** | **Psalms 17:6** |
| **1 Thessalonians 5:16-18** | |

### Verse

### Verse

Verse

Verse

**CHAPTER 2**
# BELIEVE

Whoever believes will have eternal life.

John 3:16 (NIV)

# Believe

whoever *believes* will have eternal life.

John 3:16 (NIV)

Definition — Believe

Synonyms:

Antonyms:

## Believe.

Two things that stand out when looking over the word believe:

- What it is about: To accept. To hold. To trust.
- It does not mean to disregard. Or dispute.

### NOW STOP.

**Think about it.**

Do you trust Jesus? Do you ignore God? How do you treat God?

There is so much we can already pray for and get excited for. Think about it: God wanted to save us. There isn't some list of things that need to be done to get this salvation.

God does not want anyone to perish. WOW!!

Let's praise God for this wonderful news! This is such a great thing to consider. I do not understand how people don't get hyped when they hear this. We've been offered eternal life (GUARANTEED).

# How is a man saved?

**Verse**

Romans 6:23

# ... and if we don't believe?

**Verse**

Acts 4:12

## Verse

**2 Peter 3:9**

Take time to pray over this...
Do you really believe?

When we believe in something or someone, that means we have confidence in it for very specific reasons.

To get a clearer picture, I want to dive into the word "confidence."

**Example:** You sit in a chair without checking it because you believe that it won't just collapse under your weight. You are confident in that chair.

**Think:** What are some other things you do in your day without thinking about because you have confidence in the results?

**Do you have full confidence in Jesus?**

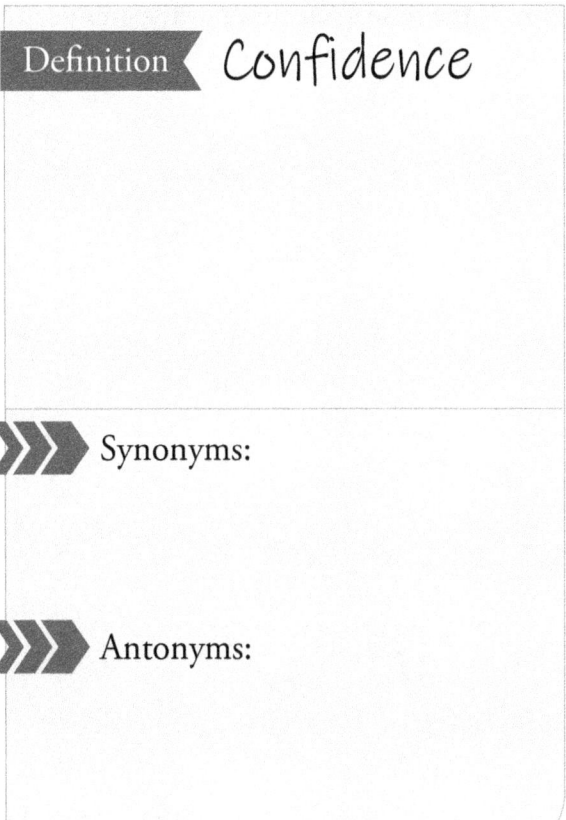

Definition — Confidence

>>> Synonyms:

>>> Antonyms:

Definition — Assurance

>>> Synonyms:

>>> Antonyms:

Do you have full confidence in the truth and reliability of the Gospel? Do you have this assurance? (If you haven't already, define assurance.) Point out specific thoughts that come into mind.

**Why are those thoughts there?**

_____
_____
_____
_____
_____
_____
_____
_____

Now is the time to create a positive mindset. Write these statements out.

I do not doubt God.

# I trust God.

*I have security in God.*

I will have confidence in God!

Believe it. Do you think your faith could be stronger? Would your life look any different if you had this strong faith? Remember, the Bible says, "Lord, help my unbelief" (Mark 9:24). Lay it all out. Please don't think something like: "Pray again? Didn't we just pray about salvation?" Go back to the statements above and decide if you can make those statements in your own life. Go back to the verses and pray over them. Spend time where it really matters!

CHAPTER 3
# PRECIOUS

Since YOU were precious in my sight, you have been honored, and I have loved you.

Isaiah 43:4 (NKJV)

## Precious

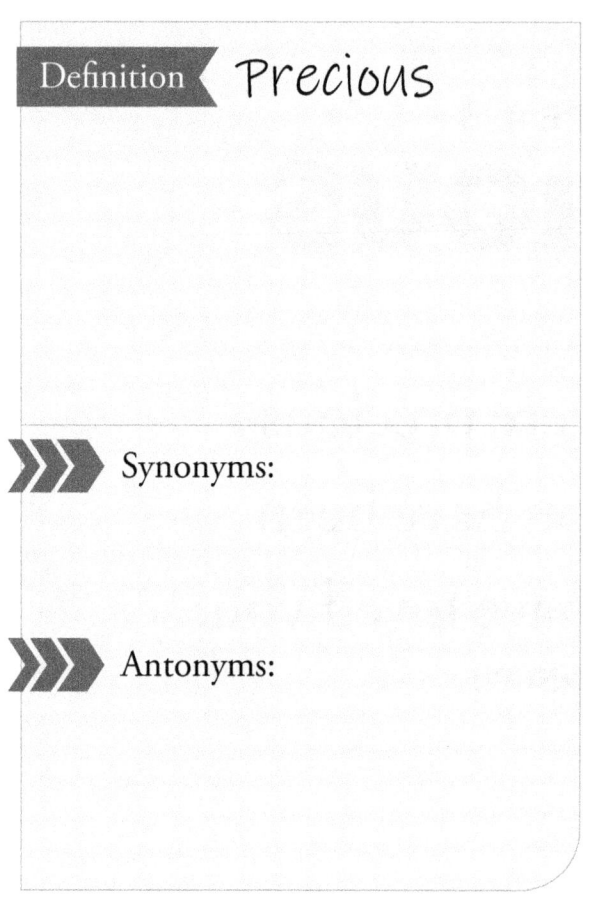

Definition: Precious

Synonyms:

Antonyms:

> Since YOU were precious in my sight, you have been honored, and I have loved you.
>
> **Isaiah 43:4 (NKJV)**

## Precious.

Stop and think. What does precious mean to you? Do you need to look it up to better understand? Look up the synonyms and antonyms of precious. Write them down.

**Did you know that God calls us precious? God. He calls US precious. He calls YOU precious.**

Do you believe God calls you precious? You are not cheap or common but cherished. We may not always feel God's love, but that doesn't mean it's not there. Will you please take some time to think about this?

**Do you think you are worth anything?** God does. He sent His only son to die for you. Yes, you. So that you wouldn't have to perish. He loves you that much!

| Precious | **Isaiah 43:4** |
|---|---|
| Treasured Possession | **Exodus 19:5** |
| Chosen | **1 Peter 2:9** |
| Child of God | **1 John 3:1** |
| Special Treasure | **Deuteronomy 7:6** |

Are you fighting against giving your life to Christ because you still want to do worldly things? What is stopping you from enjoying something so great it literally cannot have a value placed on it?

We are precious to God. We are His treasured possession. Take some time to review the verses above.

Choose one verse to write down. If you feel compelled, you have room to write more down. Pray over it. (Just talk with God. Do you believe you are precious? Ask God to make it a reality in your life.)

Verse

**Verse**

**Verse**

**CHAPTER 4**
# SET

Set your mind on things above,
not earthly things.

**Colossians 3:2 (NIV)**

# Set

> Set your mind on things above, not earthly things.
>
> **Colossians 3:2 (NIV)**

Set. That is an action verb. Whether or not we realize it, we are setting our minds on something constantly. What do you set your mind on?

If I made you listen to a song on repeat for an hour, do you think that your mind would bring that song up for the rest of the day? Most likely, it would pop up in your head.

**It is easy for our mind to go to what we spend time on. So think: What do you spend time on?**

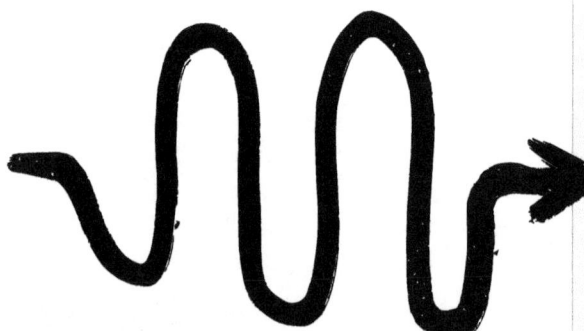

**Morning:**

**Afternoon:**

**Evening:**

Do we live our life as a chosen one of the one true God? Or do we keep living for worldly things? Are we living to serve others, to share the gospel, to praise God in our daily lives? Or are we only seeking the blessings of others? Are we pursuing the next trend, the next promotion, or the next purchase?

Look at this past week.

**What have you done?**
**What do your actions say about you?**

One thing I can tell you for sure: this world does not satisfy. You can try to pursue all these temporary highs; but in the end, you will feel empty and void of purpose and meaning.

If we truly believe and pursue a relationship with God, there is so much we are blessed with. Stop listening to the lies that are in your head—start saying these truths to yourself, truths that say you are precious, chosen, treasured children of God.

**Take some time to pray about this. Write your prayer below.**

Read Ephesians 2:19-22. When you are struggling with your identity and your purpose, think back on this.

**CHAPTER 5**
# TRANSFORMED

Be transformed by the
renewing of your mind.

**Romans 12:2 (NIV)**

# Transformed

Be <u>transformed</u> by the renewing of your mind.

**Romans 12:2 (NIV)**

**A Transformation. It means a change.**

God wants us to have a mind fixed on holiness and righteousness (Ephesians 4:23-24). We are to bring all thoughts captive so that we can obey Christ (2 Corinthians 10:4-5).

In fact, we are called to pursue righteousness, faith, love, and peace (2 Timothy 2:22)! To pursue. That doesn't mean we are going to get this passively. This is an action.

**Look up the definition of <u>pursue</u>, and don't forget to look up the antonyms.**

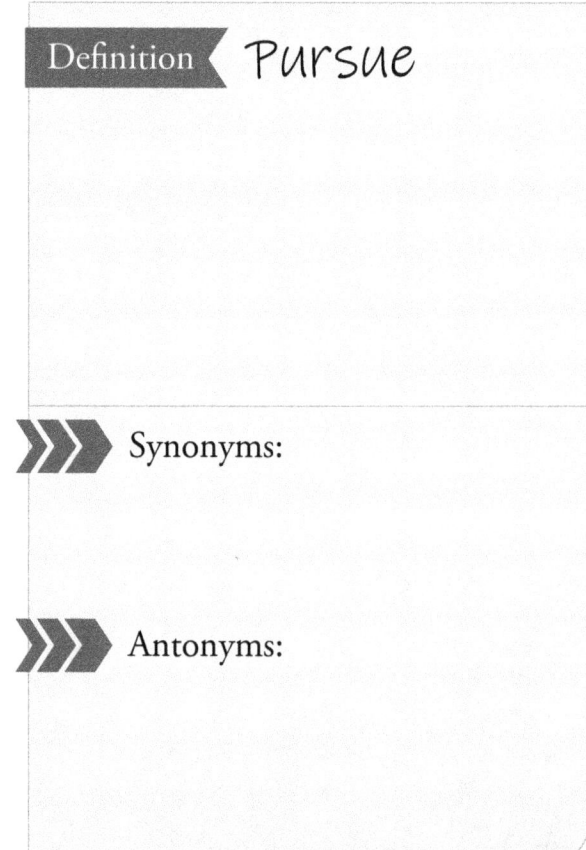

Transformed.
What does this mean to you?

Definition — Pursue

Synonyms:

Antonyms:

Does your life include daily time with God? Reading the Bible? Praying? Pursue means to strive for. If we really wanted a cookie, we aren't going to mess around with a celery stick; we are going in for the cookie.

**What do your actions say that you are currently pursuing?**

**What does your current life say about what you really want?**

_____
_____
_____
_____

### Examine:

**How much time do you spend on your phone?**

**How much time do you spend watching TV?**

**How much time do you spend complaining?**

**How much time do you spend serving others instead of yourself?**

**How much time do you spend praying?**

**How much time do you spend reading the Bible?**

Think about it: What would transformation in your life look like look like to you? Would anything change with your current habits?

_____
_____
_____
_____
_____
_____
_____
_____
_____
_____
_____

Are you pursuing God? If people around you had to give a testimony of who you are, would they say that you believe in God? Take some time to pray about this.

_____
_____
_____
_____
_____
_____
_____
_____

Now would be a great time to pray for transformation. Let's start getting rid of our worldly filth—of all worthless things. Pray to God for change.

_____
_____
_____
_____
_____
_____
_____
_____
_____

**CHAPTER 6**
# KNOW

Now this is eternal life: that they know you, the only true God, and Jesus Christ, whom you have sent.

**John 17:3 (NIV)**

## Know

Now this is eternal life: that they know you, the only true God, and Jesus Christ, whom you have sent.
**John 17:3 (NIV)**

And this is the way to have eternal life — to know you, the only true God, and Jesus Christ, the one you sent to earth.
**John 17:3 (NLT)**

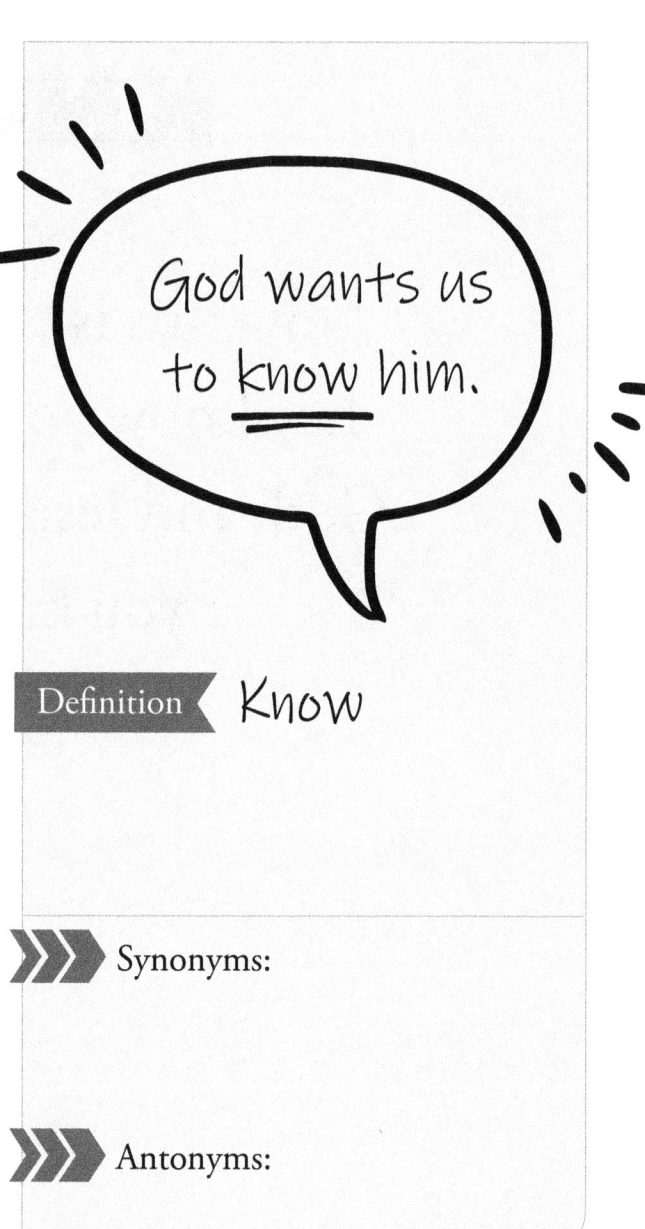

God wants us to know him.

Definition: Know

Synonyms:

Antonyms:

Great news! Your pursuit of God is not in vain. God wants you to know Him! Why would the God of the Universe want us to know Him?

**What makes anyone <u>worthy</u> to know Him?**

---

### Write it out:

**I am a sinner, but God offers me eternal life.**

**God sent Jesus to pay my debt.**

**God loves me.**

**God wants me to know Him.**

# KNOW.

**Not overlook us or treat us as peasants.**

He is King, and He won't be evasive with you. He wants you to KNOW HIM. He came to us so that we could know Him. God allows us to know and learn about Him. Do we want to know God, or is there neglect on our part? Do **we** ignore God, the King of the Universe? (Sorry if it's repetitive, but it's true!)

Do we ignore the One who created everything? Try and explain logically to yourself why you would ignore the one thing that would help you with the rest of your life. Confess and pray now. Let there be an eagerness to get close to God.

# CHAPTER 7
# GOD IS OUR FATHER

# Father

Choose a couple of verses to read and write.

| | |
|---|---|
| Isaiah 64:8 | 1 John 3:1 |
| 1 Corinthians 8:6 | Matthew 6:6 |
| Luke 12:32 | Ephesians 4:6 |

To be called a child, <u>to be **wanted**, to be considered a family member.</u> *Benson Commentary on the Bible* puts it best concerning being called a child of God: "To be accounted, acknowledged, treated by him as such, be brought so near, rendered to Him dearly, free access to Him; to be taken under his particular protection, direction, care…"[1]

Baren's notes state, "No higher love can be shown than adopting a poor, friendless orphan and giving him a parent and home… permitted to regard him as Father. When remembered how insignificant we are, to be regarded/treated as most high…"[2]

**Write this out in your own words as if God were speaking it to you.**

_____
_____
_____
_____
_____
_____
_____
_____

**Well, let's review:** The King of the World wants us as His children. How do we know this? He says that He will be a Father to us, and that we will be His sons and daughters (Galatians 3:26; 2 Corinthians 6:18). Can't argue that statement. God wants us to be a part of His family, His royal family.

He wanted to atone for our sins. To correct what we did wrong. It is about possession. God wants us. He loves us as His own children. He wants us as a part of his family. It says so in the Bible!

When we are saved, we are called children of God (1 John 3:1-2). We were adopted to sonship (Romans 8:15). The Spirit Himself testifies with our spirit that we are God's children (Romans 8:16).

> **Verse**
> God predestined us for adoption to himself.
> **Ephesians 1:5**

> **Verse**
> God calls us sons through our faith in Christ.
> **Galatians 3:26**

> **Verse**
> God gave us the right to become a child of God.
> **John 1:12**

Do you believe this? Do you believe this in your life to be the truth?

How often do you hear someone saying they want to be famous? They want to be in the "in crowd." Christians need to realize that with God, we are already promised so much more than we deserve. Why compromise being called a child of God for something that isn't even guaranteed to last a month here on Earth?

What an honor! What a gift! We could have done nothing to change or aid this outcome. All have sinned and fallen short of the glory of God (Romans 3:23). He paid our debt to deliver us (Colossians 2:14).

Why would God want people who fall short to be a part of His family/His kingdom? Because He loves us. With God, there is a personal relationship. A closeness. He isn't just someone to call on the phone once a week. Take some time to pray over this.

*See what great love the Father has lavished on us, that we should be called children of God! And that is what we are!*

**1 John 3:1a (NIV)**

## CHAPTER 8
# CARES

God wants to take
care of us.

## Cares

We are so beneath God. So unworthy. We couldn't even match up to one part of who He is. But He cares for us. God wants that title of FATHER. I don't know what your dad here on Earth is like. I know that God is still the one Father we can brag about being perfect.

To care for someone is to pay attention. To notice the small details. To see how they can be helped in situations. There is a very personal interest. It shows concern. God, who created the universe, wants to care for us humans, tiny people on a lone planet in the universe.

*God wants to take care of us.*

**Matthew 6:31-34.** Look it up and summarize it below.

_____

_____

_____

_____

**God wants to take care of you. Write it out as many times as you need for it to stick.**

*Write it out:*

**God wants to take care of me.**

**God sent Jesus to pay my debt.**

**God will take care of me.**

**God is taking care of me.**

Look up what the opposite of care is. Think about that. Take time through prayer and praise to digest what it means that God cares for you.

GOD LOVES YOU. Love. A fondness. Not a hatred. Care and concern. Not indifference. The God of the Universe LOVES you.

**Write out "God Loves Me" until it fills up the page.**

# CHAPTER 9
# GOD. ONLY GOD.

God is our God. We shall have
no other gods before Him.

**Exodus 20:2-3 (NIV)**

# God

> *God is our God. We shall have no other gods before Him.*
>
> **Exodus 20:2-3 (NIV)**

## Only God. Him First. Him Only.

May I remind you that God is omniscient (all-knowing), omnipresent (everywhere and always present), and omnipotent (all-powerful). What does it mean to have no other gods before him?

Well, consider this: What if I told you that I love the piano, a lot? But when you look at my day, there is no time spent playing a piano, or listening to a piano. There isn't even a picture of a piano anywhere in my life. Would you think I really loved the piano? Probably not.

What do you spend your time on currently? Write out what major activities you do throughout the day in the table to the right.

8:00

5:00

I strongly encourage you to choose one thing to change. Just one. It could be just to add Bible time in your day for 10 minutes somewhere. It could be stopping some of your TV time to purposely spend time with God. Write it out now. Make it a statement, a proclamation. Let it be something that you really want to do. If you don't, then start there. Pray about that.

## CHAPTER 10
# ALL POWERFUL

Behold, I am the Lord, the God of all flesh. Is **anything** too hard for me?

**Jeremiah 32:27 (ESV)**

## ALL-Powerful

**Look up the definition of <u>anything</u>.** Look up the synonyms and antonyms.

> Behold, I am the Lord, the God of all flesh. Is <u>anything</u> too hard for me?
> **Jeremiah 32:27 (ESV)**

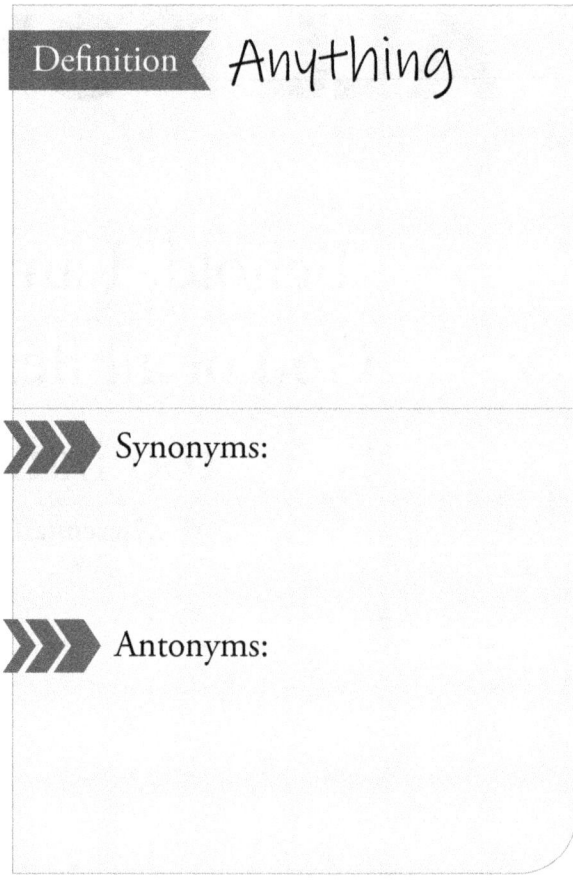

Definition: Anything

Synonyms:

Antonyms:

If you wanted anything to be done right now, what would it be?

_____

_____

_____

_____

**Do you truly believe in how capable God is?**

Now think, God can do ANYTHING. Why not trust Him with it? Think about it. Write about it now. Pray about it.

_____
_____
_____
_____
_____

God is All-Powerful. What is the opposite of powerful? Write it out.

_____
_____

Is this how you think God normally acts? DON'T GET AHEAD OF YOURSELF. We will get to God's plan for your life later. If you just jumped to a thought along the lines of, "Well then, why hasn't He…," just stop yourself there. Pull out your Bible and look up Ecclesiastes 5:2-3.

> **Verse**

**Write this out:**

*Nothing is too hard for God.*

Right now, just consider how much you may be limiting God. Do you need to limit what you are saying right now?

Verse one of Ecclesiastes 5 says the Jewish people are challenged to go to God to listen. I challenge you now to stop and listen. Make this time instead about praising God for who He is and all that He has done and can do.

**CHAPTER 11**
# SUSTAIN

He sustains **all things** by his word.

# Sustain

Read Hebrews 1:3

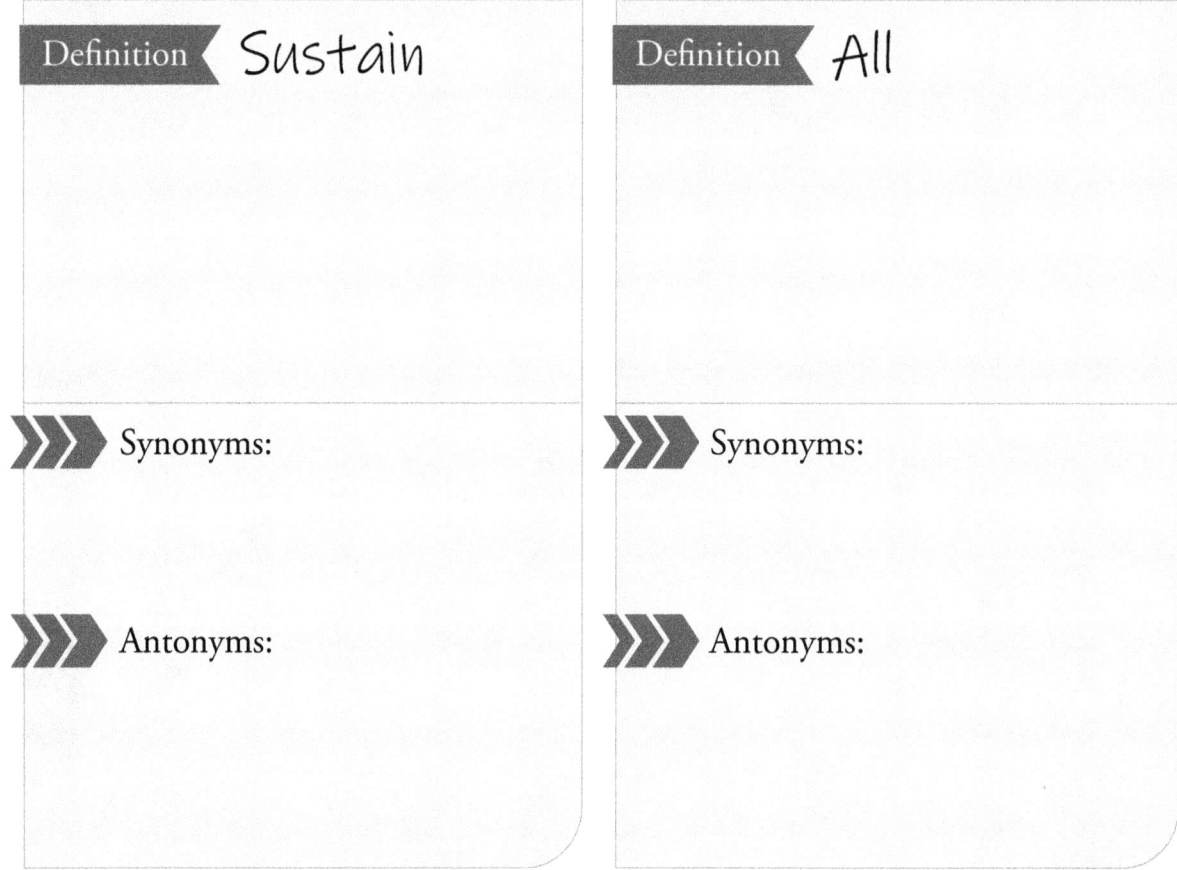

**Look up the definition of <u>sustain.</u>** Look up the synonyms and antonyms.

**Look up the definition of <u>all.</u>** Look up the synonyms and antonyms.

I love the opposites for sustain—review it. Does God do anything like that to us? No! God doesn't want to harm us. He wants to help us. To defend us. There is no hurt. It's all support—all LOVE.

Take some time to really pray and apply this in your own life. God is your sustenance, your preservation. Do you feel that way currently? If you have doubts, just start praying.

## CHAPTER 12
# FLEE

So flee youthful passions and pursue righteousness, faith, love, and peace, along with those who call on the Lord from a pure heart.

**2 Timothy 2:22 (ESV)**

# Flee

**Look up the definition of <u>flee.</u>** Look up the synonyms and antonyms.

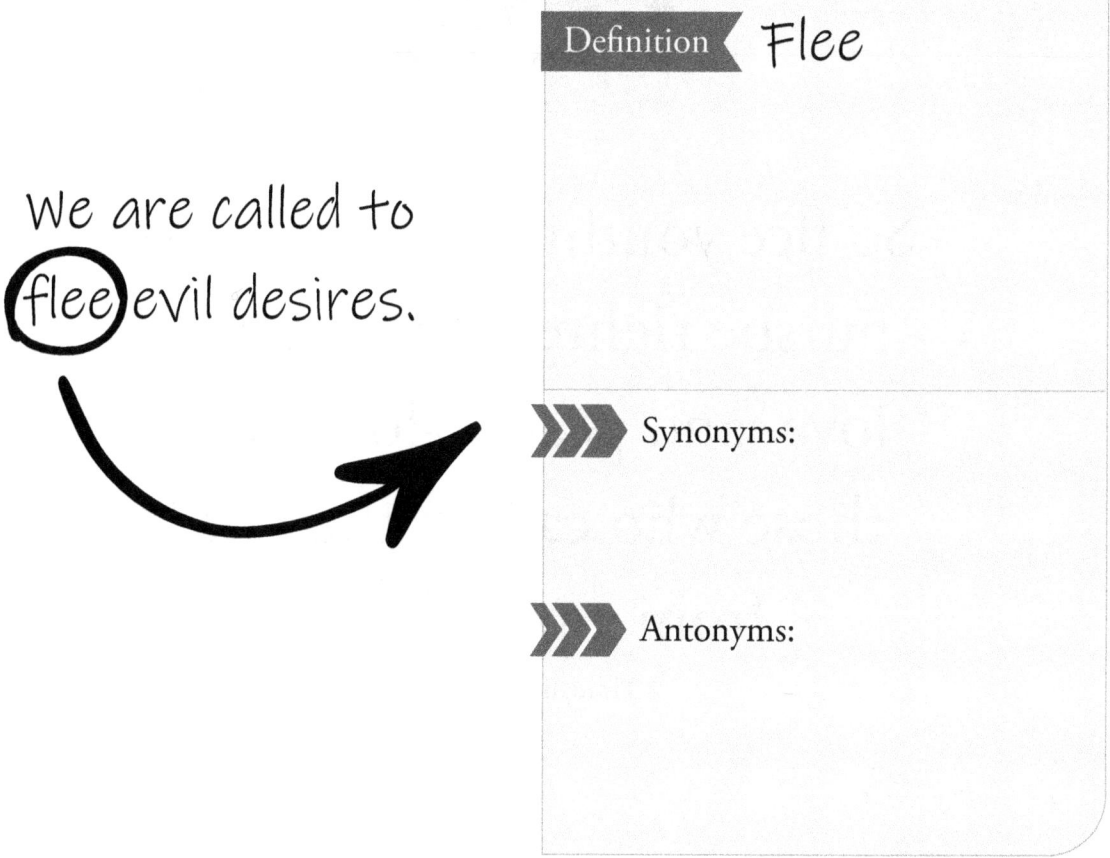

Not only that, we have goals of things that we can pursue: righteousness, faith, love, and peace (2 Timothy 2:22)! That doesn't mean we are going to get this passively. This is an action verse. It says to *pursue*.

**Think about it:** Are you fleeing from things that would make God sad? What would pursuing God look like to you?

Take time to pray over this. Make a commitment to God about your time.

**CHAPTER 13**
# ABOUND IN HOPE

May the God of hope fill you with all joy and peace in believing, so that by the power of the Holy Spirit you may abound in hope.

**Romans 15:13 (ESV)**

## Abound in Hope

> May the God of hope fill you with all joy and peace in believing, so that by the power of the Holy Spirit you may abound in hope.
>
> **Romans 15:13 (ESV)**

What's the subject about: **God.** God is described as a God of Hope.

What's the verb: **fill.** (It's an action verb).

So May God fill. **Fill YOU.**

Fill you with what? **Joy & Peace.** Not just some joy and peace. ALL Joy & peace.

### God

Described "God of Hope"

### Fill

Fill Who? You.

### Joy & Peace

Filled with ALL Joy & Peace

ABOUND IN HOPE | 65

How? In **believing**.

Believing what? God. [Reminder—God. God of hope.]

What does hope mean? Look it up and write it out.

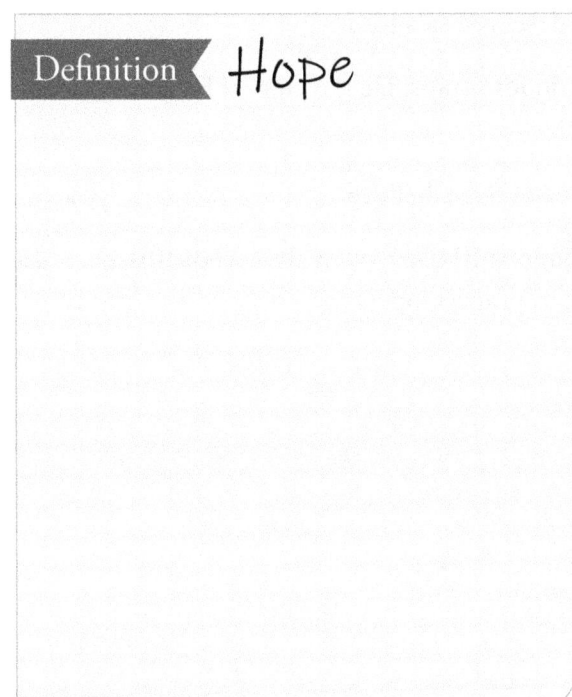

Definition — Hope

Hope is allowing one to have an assurance of something. A confidence in. An expectation of what's to happen.

We have no reason to distrust God when it tells us right here. God is a God of hope.

AND…

God wants to fill you with ALL joy and peace. We need only believe in God. God, who gives us this assurance. Why not believe when God is telling us He wants to give us these things?

Look next: What is the result of believing?

When we believe, we **ABOUND** in hope.

How? **Through the Holy Spirit.**

*Abound* sounds like an increase, right? It doesn't say maintain. Or decline. It says to abound, not lack in hope.

**God WANTS us to abound in hope.**

Definition — Abound

- Flourish in hope
- Become rich on hope
- Are well-supplied in hope
- Thrive in hope

What is this hope? Hope of what?

Of being with God one day. Knowing we are truly saved. That one day, we will be in heaven where He is. This is the hope that should fill us with joy and peace. We have nothing to worry about. The Creator of the Universe is taking care of us.

Praise God for saving us. This is an unearned, undeserved salvation.

Praise God; He doesn't make us cower. Look around for scraps. He is a God of HOPE. He wants to fill us with this joy and peace.

Do you live your life based on this idea that we need ONLY believe?

When was the last time you really thought through this? Do you truly accept this beautiful truth in your life? Take time to pray over this and to praise God.

**CHAPTER 14**

# UNITE

Christ wants to unite all things in Him.

# Unite

**Look up the definition of want.** Look up the synonyms and antonyms.

Christ <u>wants</u> to unite all things in Him.

**Definition** — Want

**Synonyms:**

**Antonyms:**

**Read Ephesians 1:7-10.**

There is so much in these verses! For now, let's focus on verse ten. This verse isn't just being written to sound good. Jesus wouldn't have died on the cross if He didn't feel strongly for us. He wants to unite—to bring us together. That is why redemption is so important. We are unholy in the face of a holy God. We needed Jesus to die on the cross for us, or we would never be able to unite with Him.

**What do you think it means to be united with God?**

_____

_____

Do you feel like you are united with God? Is there anything that can change to help you feel this way? Take some time to think and pray.

**CHAPTER 15**
# SEEK

But seek first his kingdom and his righteousness, and all these things will be given to you as well.

**Matthew 6:33 (NIV)**

## Seek

> But <u>seek</u> first his kingdom and his righteousness, and all these things will be given to you as well.
>
> **Matthew 6:33 (NIV)**

**Look up the definition of <u>seek</u>.** Look up the synonyms and antonyms.

Definition: Seek

Synonyms:

Antonyms:

God asks us to seek His kingdom first (Matthew 6:33). Is that what you do every morning? Or do you immediately jump into getting ready for work or scroll on your phone?

The man who delights in the law of the Lord is called blessed (Psalms 1:1). Can you honestly say that you delight in reading the Bible?

You are going to fit in your day what you find most valuable. You went to work because you need the cash, or you find it motivating. You talk to people because you like relationships with others. You eat/drink because your body tells you it needs sustenance. You watch TV because it interests you and because you want to relax. So, when do you read the Bible?

The Bible instructs us to meditate on it day and night so that we can follow what is written in it. Daily. DAILY people. Do you dive into the Word daily? Life and its desires can block the Bible (Mark 4:19). That is why we need it so often.

*If we aren't taking a step closer to God, we may, in fact, be stepping farther from Him.*

**(I'm not sure if someone else said this, but WHAT A STATEMENT!)**

Take some time to pray over this.

_____
_____
_____
_____
_____
_____
_____
_____
_____

# SEEK.

## What do you think seeking God in your life will look like?

**Take some time to pray over this.**

**CHAPTER 16**
# LIFE

God wants us to put our sinful nature to death so that we may live.

**Romans 8:13 (NIV)**

## Life

God wants us to put our sinful nature to death so that we may live.

Romans 8:13 (NIV)

**Life. So that we may live = have life!**

Think about it

What do you think it means to "put to death?"

**He wants to share His life with us. What an amazing gift! Simple enough—do you want life? If so, you already have the answer as to how: Pursue God daily.**

There is so much to study in the Bible. Make a point to spend time in the Word daily. Continue this, and I know you will be able to see differences in a year. Every time you read the Bible may not be rich, but I promise it will allow for growth.

"The law of the Lord is perfect, refreshing the soul" (Psalms 19:7). In this culture, I am consistently looking for a retreat; how about you? Well, here are instructions for refreshment: Read the Word of God. Our faith comes from hearing about the good news. There is so much good news packed into Scripture. We need to learn to delight in the law of the Lord. When we delight in God, He makes our steps firm (Psalms 37:23).

**Shouldn't this be enough to convince us that we need to spend more time in the Word of God? Take time to think and pray on this.**

# CHAPTER 17
# REFRESHING

The law of the Lord is
perfect, refreshing the soul.

**Psalms 19:7a (NIV)**

## Refreshing. Who needs refreshment?!

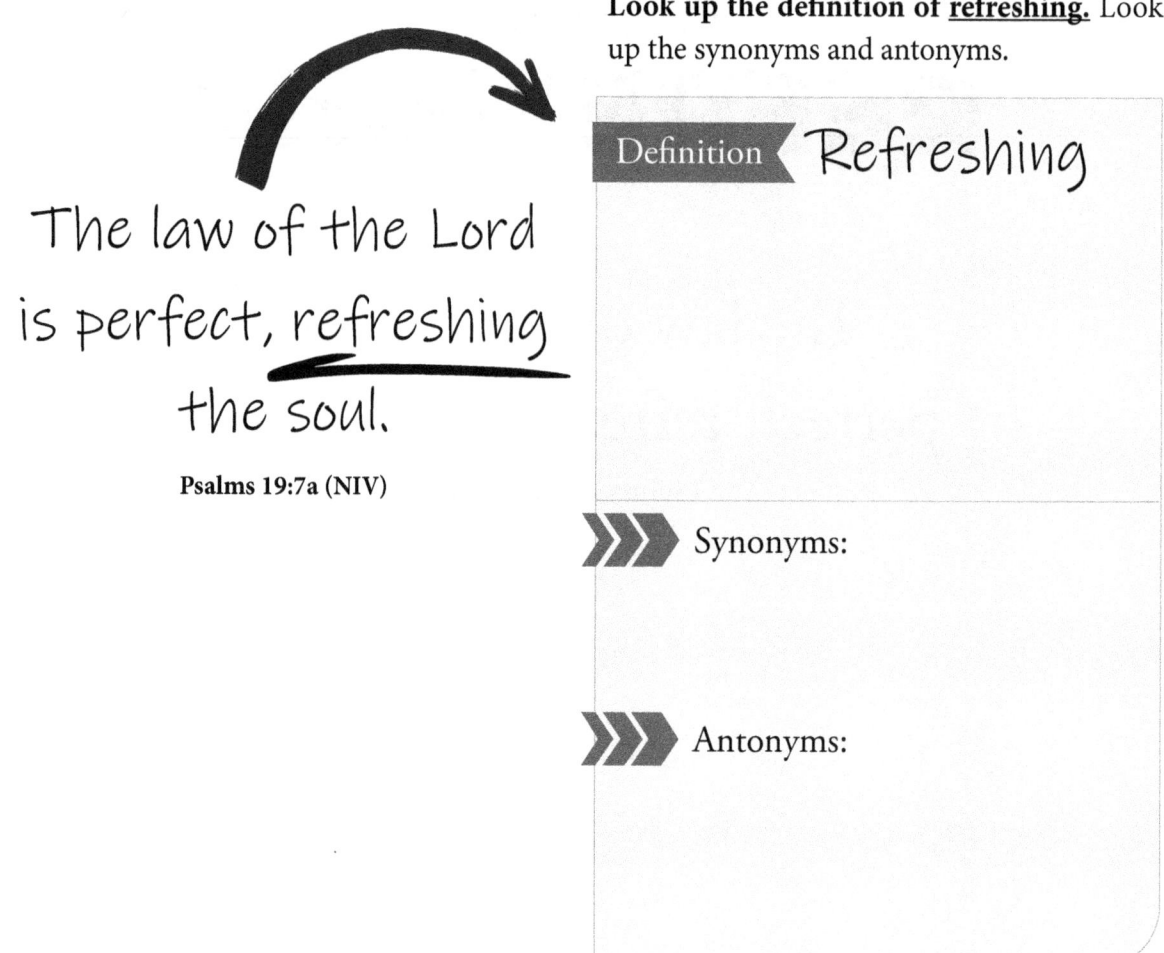

*The law of the Lord is perfect, refreshing the soul.*

**Psalms 19:7a (NIV)**

**Look up the definition of <u>refreshing</u>.** Look up the synonyms and antonyms.

| Definition | Refreshing |

>>> Synonyms:

>>> Antonyms:

What do you see as refreshing? A cold glass of water, sitting on a beach? Well here is a promised refreshment- Read the Bible. Do you see the Bible as refreshing or are you in need of a new perspective?

When we delight in God, he makes our steps firm (Psalms 37:23). Shouldn't this be enough to convince anyone to spend more time in the Word of God?

> ### Think about it
>
> **Now, remember, this isn't just checking boxes. We can't just say, "Yes! Did my five minutes in the Bible, moving on." We can't just hope that by doing the right things, we will be fine.**
>
> **If we don't trust God and seek God, we will not achieve anything. The Bible states plainly that this will be a stumbling block to anyone who does this (Romans 9:32). This is about a relationship with God.**

The Bible can be the lamp to your feet (Psalms 119:105). The Bible is the inspired Word of God; it can do a lot to assist one in growing in righteousness (2 Timothy 3:16-17). It holds truths that were shared previously and then written for everyone's benefit (1 Corinthians 2:13; 1 Thessalonians 2:13; 2 Peter 1:21).

Do you need to pray about how you view the Bible? The Bible is filled with thoughts that have been shared by God for your benefit. Write this out: God gave me the Bible for my benefit. The Bible is thoughts from God, for us, so that we know how to navigate life.

Do you need to start reading the Word more? What steps can you take today to start doing this? Think & pray over it.

_____
_____
_____
_____
_____
_____
_____
_____
_____

CHAPTER 18
# STRENGTH

The Lord is our strength.

# Strength

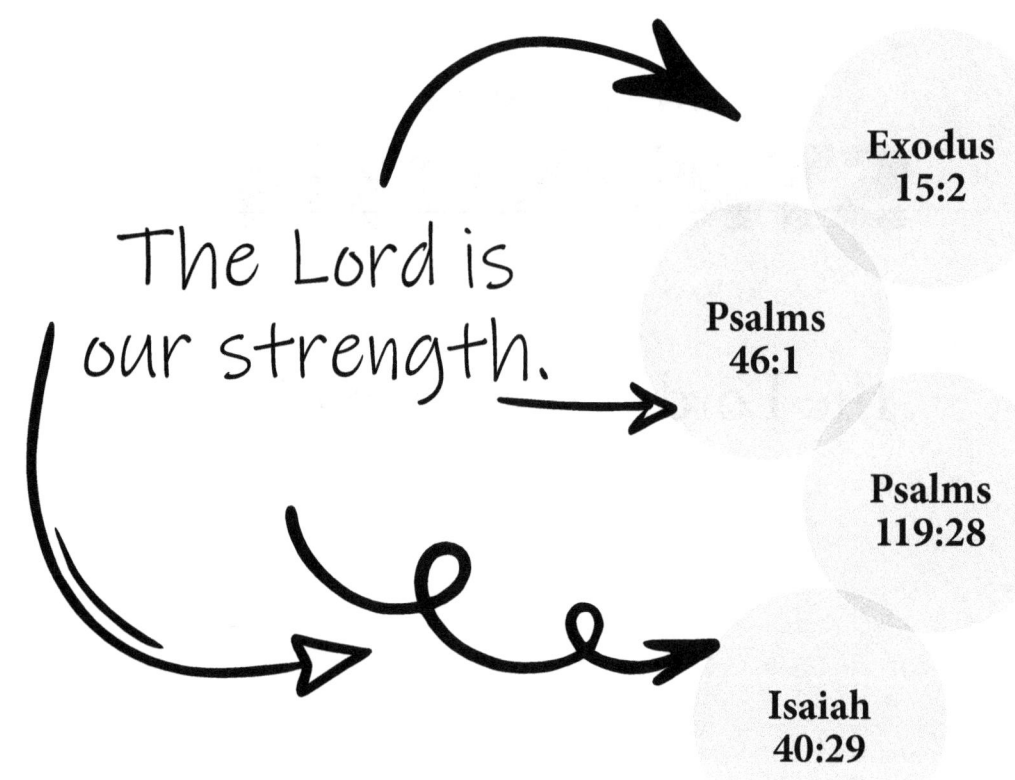

**Exodus 15:2**

**Psalms 46:1**

**Psalms 119:28**

**Isaiah 40:29**

**Look up the definition of <u>strength</u>.** Look up the synonyms and antonyms.

| Definition | Strength |
|---|---|

▶▶▶ Synonyms:

▶▶▶ Antonyms:

The Lord offers to be our strength. Did you know that?! Why do we always try to do things ourselves when the God of the universe is offering His help? **HIS STRENGTH.**

With God, we can have stability and security no matter the situation. Without Him, it's chaos. We are powerless without Him. We are weak.

**Would things be different if you lived knowing God is your strength? How?**

Invite God to be your strength now if you haven't already. Admit that you cannot do it on your own. Admit your own weakness and invite God in to work in amazing ways.

# CHAPTER 19
# TRUST

*The LORD is my strength and my shield; my heart trusts in him, and he helps me. My heart leaps for joy, and with my song I praise him.*

**Psalms 28:7 (NIV)**

## Trust

> The LORD is my strength and my shield; my heart trusts in him, and he helps me. My heart leaps for joy, and with my song I praise him.
> **Psalms 28:7 (NIV)**

> The LORD is my strength and my [impenetrable] shield; My heart trusts [with unwavering confidence] in Him, and I am helped; Therefore, my heart greatly rejoices, And with my song I shall thank Him and praise Him.
> **Amplified**

Here it is. If you truly are trusting God to be your strength, look at what it tells us will happen. God will help us! More people would trust a chair to hold them when they sit down, and that is man-made. God is so much more than man. So stop saying you trust Him. Really apply it to your life. I imagine it will make a difference. Do you trust Him with unwavering confidence? Or is there doubt?

**Write this verse out as if you were telling God this yourself. Take time to pray.**

Verse

# CHAPTER 20
# CAST

Cast all your anxiety on him because he cares for you.

**1 Peter 5:7 (NIV)**

# Cast

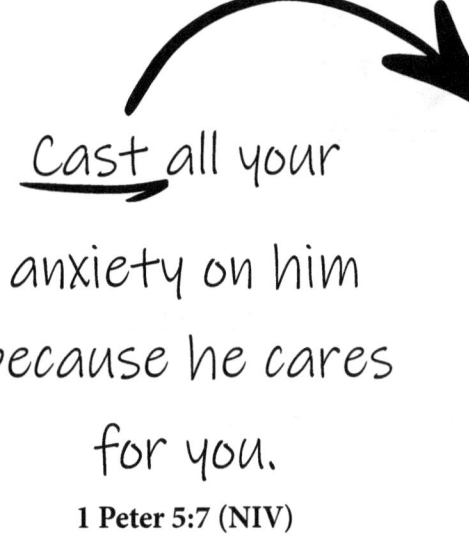

*Cast all your anxiety on him because he cares for you.*
**1 Peter 5:7 (NIV)**

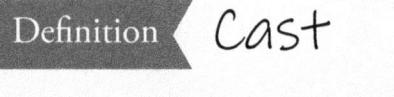

Definition **Cast**

*To throw away, to hurl*

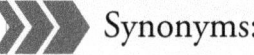

Synonyms:
*Eject, hurl, heave, project*

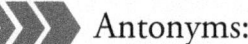

Antonyms:
*To keep; retain*

**The Bible tells us to CAST all our anxieties on Him.**

Cast—that's an action verb! Do you need to look it up? Cast means to throw away from you.

Think about this. Do you cast away your anxiety? Or does it fester in your thoughts? People tend to hold on to anxiety, complain about it to others, and stress over it continually.

Guess what? God gives us an out! He just tells us to give it to Him. To let go. Lay it at His feet in prayer. This is a great way to trust God. Prayer is so crucial. Until we take time to stop ourselves from acting on what we know, the weight that we carry will never leave; it will overwhelm us. This is where burnout, breakdown, and a negative mood all set in; we try to rely on ourselves, our own capabilities to handle the concern. God wants to help; He asks that you just entrust it to Him in prayer.

God offers to give you strength. To be your refuge (Psalm 46:1). God wants to help you (Psalms 121:1-2). He is watching over you (Genesis 28:15). The Bible states that God will be with you wherever you go (Joshua 1:9). That is how you can cast your anxiety away. Start focusing on the truth!

> ### Think about it
>
> **Can you tell when there are times in your life when you are more anxious, or easily angered?** Maybe there is more bitterness than thankfulness coming out of your mouth? That would be a good time to analyze how much time you are spending in God's Word. The more our mood gets sour, the more likely we aren't focused on God, or His work, promises or love.
>
> The more we draw near to God, He will come near to us.

**Take some time to write out these truths to yourself.**

God is my strength.
_____
_____

God is my refuge.
_____
_____

God is my help.
_____
_____

God is my watching over me.
_____
_____

God cares for me.
_____
_____

If you need time to confess to God, do it now.

# CHAPTER 21
# SHAKEN

Cast your cares on the Lord and he will sustain you; he will never let the righteous be shaken.

**Psalms 55:22 (NIV)**

## Shaken

> Cast your cares on the Lord and he will <u>sustain</u> you he will never let the righteous be <u>shaken</u>.
>
> **Psalm 55:22 (NIV)**

**Look up the definition of <u>sustain</u>.** Look up the synonyms and antonyms.

Definition — Sustain

>>> Synonyms:

>>> Antonyms:

**Look up the definition of <u>shaken</u>.** Look up the synonyms and antonyms.

Definition — Shaken

>>> Synonyms:

>>> Antonyms:

**Do you feel shaken?** Go back and read the definition if needed. God cares for us. In Him, we can be confident! He is ready and able to help when we go to Him in prayer (Hebrews 4:14-16). Jesus has been through it all. Think about Jesus' life span on Earth: His family doubted Him, people plotted to kill Him, He was mocked, spat on, rejected, and even abandoned by His disciples. People opposed Him, and He was able to endure (Hebrews 12:3).

Imagine going through that! What would your attitude be like?

**God can and will help us if we reach out to Him.** He is not a genie in a bottle who grants wishes. He does have a perfect plan, though. If something isn't going the way you want, maybe there is a reason. Maybe there is something better. Take time to pray over this. Confess your doubts. Give it to God.

> God is in control! GOD WILL HELP ME. I am confident that God will supply my EVERY need.

Write it out:

# CHAPTER 22
# PEACE

God's peace will surround us through prayer.

**Philippians 4:4-7 (NIV)**

## Peace

God's <u>peace</u> will <u>surround</u> us through prayer.

**Philippians 4:4-7 (NIV)**

*Write it out!*

**Look up the definition of <u>surround</u>.**

Definition — Surround

**Look up the definition of <u>peace.</u>** Look up the synonyms and antonyms.

**Definition** *Peace*

▶▶ Synonyms:

▶▶ Antonyms:

Why would God allow this for us? We have done nothing for Him and can do nothing for him. With Jesus, we can have peace with God because it is a GIFT given to us through justification (Romans 5:1).

This world is full of so much that upsets us. Look at all the antonyms of peace. Does any of that seem familiar when looking at society? Do you need some deliverance?

We don't need to be bogged down any more than necessary. We can be made alive in Christ (Ephesians 2:4-5). We don't know what will happen tomorrow (James 4:13-16). I say you try trusting Jesus completely. I mean, He already knows what is going to happen. Why not let Him be our comfort (2 Corinthians 1:4-5)?

**Take some time to imagine what your life would be like if you were "Alive in Christ."**

**Would there be any differences? Would you still have worry? Anxiety? Pray.**

_____
_____
_____
_____
_____

*What hope we have in Jesus!*

CHAPTER 23
# FOCUS

You keep him in perfect peace whose mind is stayed on you, because he trusts in you.

Isaiah 26:3 (NIV)

# Focus

> You keep him in <u>perfect</u> peace whose mind is stayed on you, because he <u>trusts</u> in you.
>
> Isaiah 26:3 (NIV)

**Look up the definition of <u>perfect</u>.** Look up the synonyms and antonyms.

**Look up the definition of <u>focused</u>.** Look up the synonyms and antonyms.

Definition: Perfect

>>> Synonyms:

>>> Antonyms:

Definition: Focused

>>> Synonyms:

>>> Antonyms:

Stop and take a minute to think about your day. What do you spend your time on? What you spend your time on is usually where your focus is. Here is an example:

**How much time does God get?**

- Work
- Phone
- Food
- TV
- Sleep
- Bible

Is God the spotlight of your life? Is He behind how you act? We can still work and glorify God through our work. Are we really working with this mindset?

I love that the Bible gives it to us simply.

**Want peace? Focus on God.** How can you do that today? Is there anything you can take some time from to have more time with God? We need to check in on our activities regularly.

_____
_____
_____
_____

**Thoughts:**
- ☐ Read the Bible
- ☐ Put on some worship music and sing
- ☐ Pray

**Make a commitment now.** Choose to find time for God. Plan out some different ways you can. Plan ways to keep you accountable (alarms, buddy system). Ask God for help. Admit your weakness. Lay it all before Him and ask Him to work in you.

_____
_____
_____
_____
_____

Can you look at your own life and see what you do when you come across a difficult situation? Pray over it. Use these verses to guide you in prayer.

**Verse**

**Verse**

# CHAPTER 24
# WATCH PRESERVE

The Lord will watch over your coming and going both now and forevermore.

**Psalms 121:8 (NIV)**

## Watch. Preserve.

**Definition** Watch

The Lord will watch over your coming and going both now and forevermore.

**Psalms 121:8 (NIV)**

▶▶▶ Synonyms:

▶▶▶ Antonyms:

**Definition** Preserve

▶▶▶ Synonyms:

▶▶▶ Antonyms:

The Lord shall preserve thy going out and thy coming in from this time forth, and even for evermore.

**Psalms 121:8 (KJV)**

**Read the definition of watch and preserve.**

Did you know that we are told God keeps watch over us? Read the definition carefully. Look at what watch is not—it does not mean we are ignored or neglected. God wants to protect us, not abandon us! Do you feel that way? Why or why not?

_____

_____

_____

Now, if I am being completely honest, I felt like I was overlooked for a long time by God. I didn't feel like I was getting the close personal attention I thought I would get. How blinded was I?!

God doesn't just leave us to figure things out. He is watching over us. He has plans and direction for us (Proverbs 3:6; 16:3; Psalms 32:8). We are told to be still and wait on Him (Psalms 27:14; 37:7). (More on these later!) He will come to save us (Isaiah 35:4). Remember, He sees us as His children. Think: He is a GOOD Father. Do you think He would leave you to yourself if He were a good father who loves and cares for you?

**Write these out so you can start to believe it!**

God is watching over me.

_____

God has a plan for me.

_____

If I follow, He will lead me and guide me.

_____

I need to be still and wait on the Lord.

_____

He will come to save me.

_____

**Need time to praise God?** Do it now.

**CHAPTER 25**

# RESTORES

He restores my soul.

Psalms 23:3 (ESV)

# Restores

**He restores their soul.**

Hallelujah! Do you need restoration? I need restoration.

Imagine the feeling of being restored. Made new. To recover, rehabilitate. To renew.

I don't know about you, but I'll admit that I am damaged. I am broken and in serious need of repair.

**But God RESTORES.**

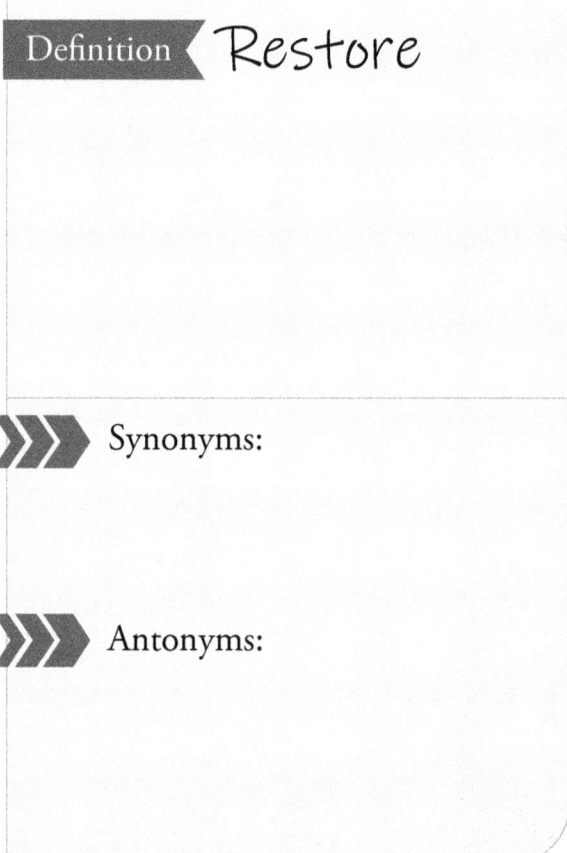

It doesn't say He will harm or hurt us. It talks about restoration and healing.

**Think about this. Do you believe God will do this for you?**

Read Psalms 23. Think about how this can impact your life if you allow God to work. God is with us; He leads us on paths of righteousness. That doesn't mean life will be easy. This Psalm very clearly tells us this. All we know is that there is a valley of the shadow of death. These paths aren't in sunny valleys or with rainbows. No, it says that we could very well be walking through the shadow of death. We don't need to fear, though, because God is our shepherd. He is with us.

## moment of jaw drop

Yes. In the darkest valley, you are called to trust in God. When you can see nothing, all you can do is have faith. Faith that God will take care of you and provide for you.

## Faith is all God asks of you. How great is that?!

I am so appreciative that God doesn't ask for a list of specifics from us in order for us to receive His blessings.

**CHAPTER 26**
# FAITHFUL

God is Faithful.

# Faithful

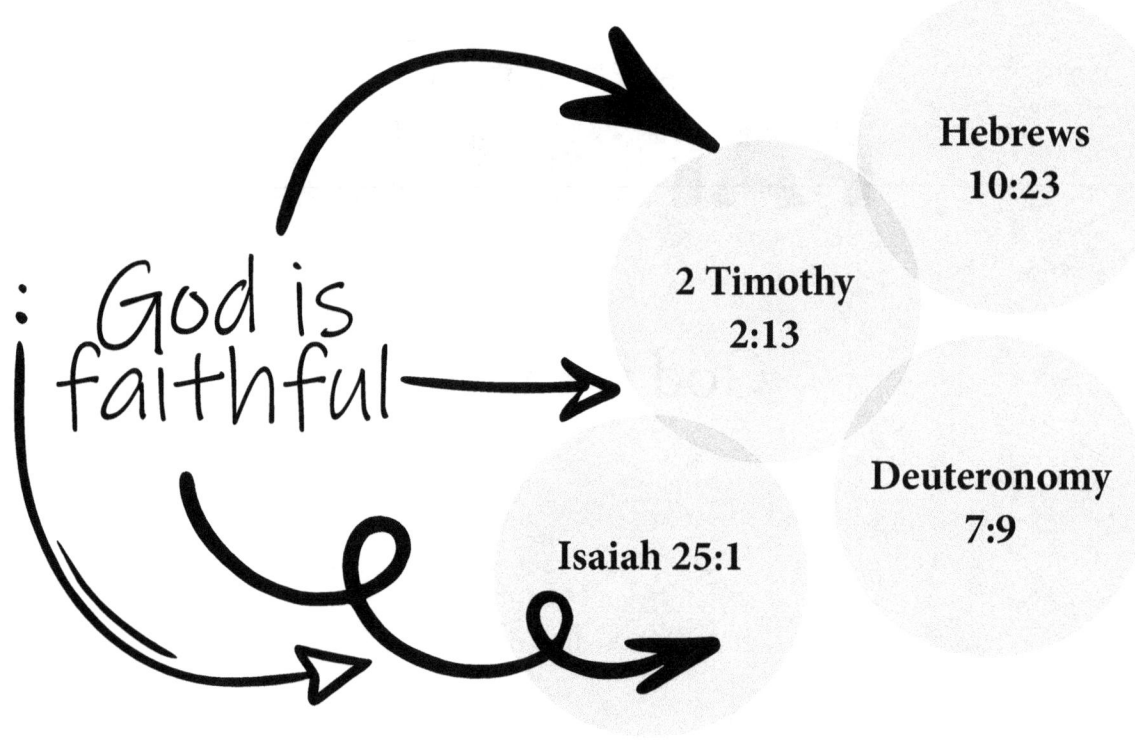

**Hebrews 10:23**

**2 Timothy 2:13**

**Deuteronomy 7:9**

**Isaiah 25:1**

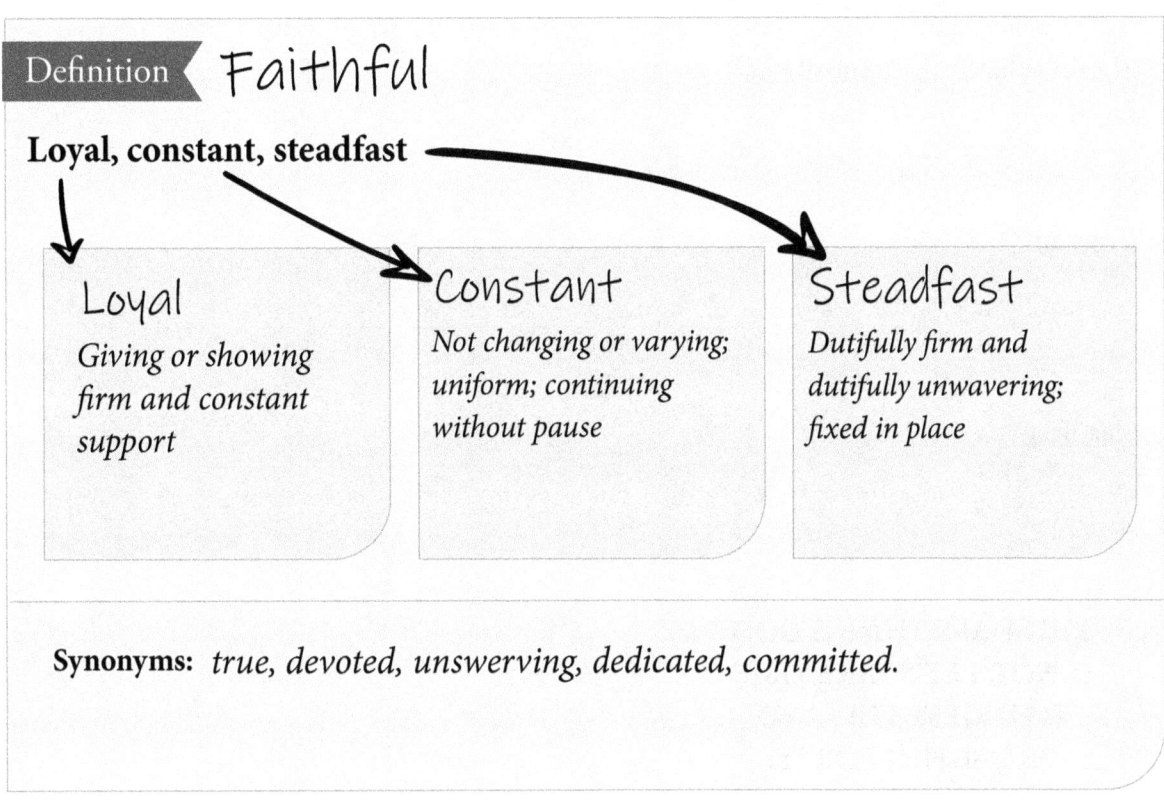

**Praise God. He IS FAITHFUL!** He doesn't change. He is unwavering. The God of the Universe—He is faithful to you. Why? Because He loves you. That's it. He just loves us. Thank you, God, for this wonderful gift! Take time to pray over this. Take time to thank God for what He isn't, too. (IE: He isn't changing!)

Think: What is the **opposite** of Loyal?

Constant?

Steadfast?

> **THESE ARE THINGS GOD IS NOT. LET'S TAKE TIME TO DIGEST THIS AND PRAISE HIM FOR IT!**

**CHAPTER 27**
# PRICELESS

How priceless is your
unfailing love.

# Priceless

How Priceless is your unfailing love (NIV)

How **precious** is your steadfast love (ESV)

How **precious** is your loving devotion (BSB)

How **excellent** is thy loving kindness (KJV)

How **precious** is your gracious love (ISV)

All people may take refuge in the shadow of your wings.

**Psalms 36:7 (NIV)**

**Look up the definition of priceless.** Look up the synonyms and antonyms.

**Definition** Priceless

Synonyms:

Antonyms:

**Look up the definition of precious.** Look up the synonyms and antonyms.

**Definition** Precious

Synonyms:

Antonyms:

How amazing! There is so much to go over. Be patient with me. Let's start with priceless.

Think about something that is considered priceless in your life. You can tell it's priceless because you don't want to go through life without it. You will spend a lot of time guarding it.

Now think, do you treat God's love as priceless? As something irreplaceable in your life? Or are you just spending time with Him when it is convenient for you? Do you treat God's love as precious?

Read the definition of precious: Not to be treated carelessly. Do you pay attention to God? Are you very attentive to how He fits in your life, or are you not even considering Him in your daily life? How about your plans?

**Be honest and real with God now.**

Next, look at how God's love is characterized. Steadfast. Gracious.

Though it is beyond your comprehension, God's love is steadfast. (Go define steadfast now.) God's love is unwavering, fixed, and unhesitating towards you. He has a love that is resolute and unchanging. **This has never depended on you.** "While we were still sinners, Christ died for us (Romans 5:8)."

Here are some antonyms of steadfast: dishonest, disloyal, false, flexible. Praise God that He **isn't** unreliable. God is unwavering in His love for you. Do you truly believe this? Review the definition of **steadfast**. Take some time to write and pray about it.

> Definition: Steadfast

Before you move on, you need to look closely at the second part of the verse. Go back and read it again.

God allows us to take refuge in His presence, not under His angels or random helpers. Under God's wings, we can have refuge.

Think: What is a refuge? Read the definition. What is a sanctuary or hideaway?

> **Definition** *Refuge*
>
> *Condition of being safe or sheltered from pursuit, danger, trouble*
>
> ⟫ Synonyms:
> *Protection, security, sanctuary, hideaway*
>
> ⟫ Antonyms:
> *exposed, hazard, entrance, out in danger's way*

**Why would someone go to one of those places? What is its use?**

Does that sound like a place you want to be today? Pray about this.

# CHAPTER 28
# COMPARED TO GOD

Many, O LORD my God, are the wonders You have done, and the plans You have for us—none can compare to You—if I proclaim and declare them, they are more than I can count..

Psalms 40:5 (BSB)

## Compared to God

*Blessed is the man who has made the Lord his trust.*

Many, O LORD my God, are the wonders You have done, and the plans You have for us—none can compare to You—if I proclaim and declare them, they are more than I can count..

**Psalms 40:4-5 (BSB)**

### None can compare to God.

Write that out.

**Nothing can compare to God!**

**How could we not trust him?** Take some time to go through these verses. Write them out. Pray over them.

| | |
|---|---|
| **Job 5:9** | **Job 9:10** |
| **Romans 11:33** | **Job 37:5** |
| **Psalms 136:4** | |

**Verse**

_____
_____
_____
_____
_____

**Verse**

_____
_____
_____
_____
_____

**Verse**

**Verse**

Now the hard question: Do you really believe nothing can compare to God? Where is the time spent in your day? (*think – how about those TV shows that you NEED to catch?*)

Take time to reflect on just how amazing God is. He created the universe! There is truly nothing better than him.

# CHAPTER 29
# PLAN

## God made us. We are His.

**Psalms 100:3 (NIV)**

# Plan

God made us. We are His.
Psalms 100:3

God has a plan for you.
Jeremiah 29:11

He set you apart before you were born.
Galatians 1:15

Before God formed you in the womb, He knew you.
Jeremiah 1:5

Do you feel like sometimes there is just no direction to your life? While this may feel true, that doesn't make it a fact. I've said it before, and I will say it again,

"God has a plan for you." Write out Jeremiah 29:11.

**Verse**

Do you think God has a plan for you? What is your reasoning for that?

God has plans in which we flourish. Look up the definition of prosper. It's all there. It very clearly states God doesn't want to harm you but to help you. This is in the Bible, the Word of God. He chose to have this in there for a reason. Read Jeremiah 1:5 again. God doesn't have a plan for only some people in this world. He has a plan for everyone—that means you! Do you accept this in your heart? Take time to think and pray on this.

# CHAPTER 30
# PROSPER

For I know the plans I have for you …
plans to prosper you and not to harm you,
plans to give you hope and a future.

**Jeremiah 29:11 (NIV)**

## To Prosper

*For I know the plans I have for you...*

**Definition** — Plan

Synonyms:

Antonyms:

*Plans to prosper you and not to harm you,*

**Definition** — Prosper

Synonyms:

Antonyms:

*Plans to give you hope and a future.*

**Jeremiah 29:11 (NIV)**

**Definition** — Hope

Synonyms:

Antonyms:

Grasp this: The person who made everything thing has a plan for you that allows you to prosper. (Think: A plan that is not set up for failure.)

> We know that this person has NEVER failed. Will never fail. We know this person is loving. Faithful. Unchanging.
>
> This is GOD! He knows the future. Our future!
>
> Why would you walk away thinking you know better?

Take time to think and pray on this.

# CHAPTER 31
# ABANDON

> Keep your lives free from the love of money and be content with what you have, because God has said, "Never will I leave you; never will I forsake you."
>
> **Hebrews 13:5 (NIV)**

## Abandon

Let's Compare Hebrews 13:5

**Hebrews 13:5 (NIV)** ↔ **Hebrews 13:5 (NLT)**

Keep your lives free from the love of money...

And be content with what you have...

Because God has said, "Never will I leave you; never will I forsake you."

Don't love money...

be satisfied with what you have...

For God has said, "I will never fail you. I will never abandon you."

Think: God will never desert you.

God—the One who created the universe, will never leave you. Do you accept this as truth in your life?

# NEVER.
# At NO time.
# Not ever.
# Not at all.
# Not in any way.

**God will <u>never abandon</u> you.**

**God will never desert you.**

**God will remain with you.**

**God will stay with you.**

**God will keep you.**

Definition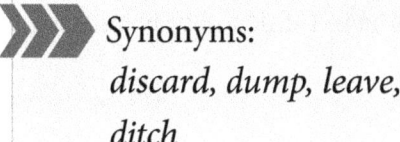

Synonyms:
*discard, dump, leave, ditch*

Antonyms:
*hold, keep, preserve, maintain, defend, support, pursue*

**Rewrite Hebrews 13:5.**

> Verse

Now pause. Read the opposite of abandon (similar to desert). We know that God will preserve you. Read Psalms 121:7-8. How does that make you feel?

Take time to think and pray on this.

# CHAPTER 32
# TO BE AFRAID

So we say with confidence, "The Lord is my helper; I will not be afraid. What can mere mortals do to me?"

**Hebrews 13:6 (NIV)**

## To Be Afraid

> So we say with confidence, "The Lord is my helper; I will not be afraid. What can mere mortals do to me?"
> Hebrews 13:6 (NIV)

**Look up the definition of afraid.** Look up the synonyms and antonyms.

Definition — **Afraid**

>> Synonyms:

>> Antonyms:

The NLT says, "The Lord is my helper, so I will have no fear."

The NKJV states that since God is our helper, "I will not fear." This is a firm statement.

God is your helper. Don't fear.

The best part of this is knowing how we should be. If we are not to be afraid, what are we to be? Look at the antonyms. Write over each word.

Bold

Courageous

Calm

Composed

Happy

Eager

> **Recap**
>
> Who is my <u>helper?</u>
>
> The Lord
>
> The King of the Universe
>
> The Mighty One
>
> The Prince of Peace
>
> The Way
>
> The Life
>
> The Saviour of the World
>
> Alpha & Omega
>
> Mighty God
>
> Counselor
>
> Redeemer
>
> Light of the World
>
> Living God
>
> Messiah
>
> Everlasting Father

Take time to praise God and pray over any shortcomings you may have when trusting Him.

_____
_____
_____
_____
_____
_____
_____

Additional Verses to enjoy:

| Luke 1:37 | Hebrews 1:3 | Mark 10:27 |
|---|---|---|
| Jeremiah 32:17 | Psalms 147:5 | Isaiah 40:28 |
| Job 42:1-2 | Ephesians 3:20 | Isaiah 43:13 |
| Ephesians 1:19 | Genesis 18:14 | Matthew 19:26 |

## Verse

_____
_____
_____
_____

**Verse**

**Verse**

**Verse**

**Verse**

## CHAPTER 33
# IT IS GOOD

# It is Good

**Psalms 73:28**

Look it up and summarize it below. *(For additional enjoyment, read it in different Bible translations.)*

> Verse

# IT IS GOOD | 149

**(NIV)**
It is <u>good</u> to be near God...

**Definition: Good**
*to be desired or approved of; satisfactory in quality; excellent*

 Synonyms:

 Antonyms:

---

**(BSB)**
To <u>draw</u> <u>Near</u> to God

**Definition: Draw near**
*to get close to, approach, come closer*

 Antonyms:

---

**(ESV)**
I have made the Lord God my <u>Refuge</u>

**Definition: Refuge**
*condition of being safe or sheltered from pursuit, danger, or trouble*

 Synonyms:

 Antonyms:

How do you feel when you approach God?

Do you feel different when you walk away?

Do you truly see God as your Refuge? Your help?

Take time now to pray about this.

**CHAPTER 34**

# HIS DIVINE POWER

His divine power has given us everything we need for a godly life.

2 Peter 1:3 (NIV)

## His Divine Power

*His divine power has given us everything we need for a godly life.*
**2 Peter 1:3 (NIV)**

**Power**

Whose power? God's.

**Gives**

Gives who? You.

**Everything**

Everything? We need for a godly life.

### Recap

Let's talk about this. God:

- who owes us nothing
- who created the universe.

God wants to share his power with us.

Why? He wants to supply our every need for living a godly life.

How amazing is this? He isn't leaving us high and dry. We aren't left searching, trying to figure out what to do. He wants to help us. Instead of struggling on our own, He wants to strengthen us. Wow. But it goes on. Look up the rest of the 2 Peter 1:3 and write it out.

> **Verse**

You can receive all things by coming to know God.

- God can be known.
- He wants to be known.
- He wants you to come to Him.
- He is willing to share so much with you.

Take time now to pray about this.

# CHAPTER 35
# REJOICE, PRAY, & GIVE THANKS

# Rejoice, Pray, & Give Thanks.

*Rejoice always...* →

**Definition: Always**
every time, on every occasion, without exception.

▶▶▶ Synonyms:

▶▶▶ Antonyms:

*...pray without ceasing, give thanks in all circumstances; for this is the will of God in Christ Jesus for you.*
1 Thessalonians 5:16-18 (ESV)

**Definition: Without Ceasing**
not coming to an end; no stopping

▶▶▶ Synonyms:

▶▶▶ Antonyms:

# REJOICE, PRAY, & GIVE THANKS | 157

God doesn't just want to help us from afar; He wants to hear from us.

## The Bible tells us:

To rejoice when?

When should we pray?

To give thanks when?

When someone is grateful, they are full of thanks, expressing gratitude.

**How can we express gratitude to God Right <u>Now</u>?**
**<u>Count</u> the blessings in your life.**

_____
_____
_____
_____
_____
_____
_____
_____
_____

There is so much we can be thankful for being a believer in Christ. Do you need to review what we've talked about thus far? God is a caring God. He loves us so much that He sent His son to die for us. God wants to give us eternal life. He wants a relationship with us (more to come on this!). He helps us as we go through life. Don't just take these for granted. This isn't something that we deserve or that should happen. He wants it to happen. He wants us to always rejoice, pray all the time, and continually thank Him. Now is a perfect time to do just that!

# CHAPTER 36
# BE STILL

# Be Still

| Psalms 46:10 | Exodus 14:14 | 1 Samuel 12:16 |
|---|---|---|
| Exodus 14:14 | Psalms 37:7 | Isaiah 40:31 |

What is another way to say, "Be still"?

# BE STILL | 161

**Look up the definition of <u>still</u> and <u>know</u>.** Look up their synonyms and antonyms.

Definition — Still

Synonyms:

Antonyms:

We hear it: "Be still and know that I am God." Okay. Now what? Well, how do we define still?

When we are told to be still, we are told to quiet down, to remain in a place or to be at rest, to become motionless. Still's synonyms are great: compose, settle, calm, fixed. Does that sound like us when we are stressed?

What is the opposite of still?

What "be still" doesn't mean is to be broken, changeable, unfixed, stirred, agitated.

YIKES. That sounds more like me.

We are told to be still and know that He is God. We talked about this briefly before, but let's review what it means to know. Write it out.

Definition — Know

Synonyms:

Antonyms:

In difficult times, what about God are we supposed to know?

Do you feel like you can know God? Why or why not?

Here are some things to remember when we are blinded by a difficult situation:

Go back to those verses. Take some time to write it out and think over a few.

| Verse |
|---|
|  |

_____
_____
_____
_____
_____

**Verse**

**Verse**

**Verse**

## God isn't complicated.

I hope and pray this book gives you plenty of opportunity to BE STILL AND KNOW.

## Endnotes

[1] Benson, Rev. Joseph. 1847. Joseph Benson's Commentary on the Old and New Testaments. G. Lane & C.B. Tippett.

[2] Barnes, Albert. Albert Barnes' Notes on the Bible. Bible Hub, October 2024.

# About the Author

## Alyssa Rueter

Alyssa Rueter was born in Illinois but made Texas her home after moving there for graduate school—and meeting her husband. While pursuing a career in Athletic Training, she discovered her deeper passion: learning about God and helping others engage with Scripture.

Through years of leading Bible study groups and conversations with fellow believers, she realized that many people struggle to articulate what they truly know about God. This realization inspired her to write this book—to help others discover how great God is and to experience the indescribable joy that comes from having a relationship with Him.

www.ingramcontent.com/pod-product-compliance
Lightning Source LLC
LaVergne TN
LVHW061253060426
835507LV00020B/2310